CAMBRIDGE LIBRARY COLLECTION

Books of enduring scholarly value

History

The books reissued in this series include accounts of historical events and movements by eye-witnesses and contemporaries, as well as landmark studies that assembled significant source materials or developed new historiographical methods. The series includes work in social, political and military history on a wide range of periods and regions, giving modern scholars ready access to influential publications of the past.

The History of Contract Labor in the Hawaiian Islands

Katharine Coman (1857–1915) was an American historian and economist who served as professor and later dean at Wellesley College. Her works include *A History of England* (1899), *Economic Beginnings of the Far West* (1912), and this 1903 monograph. Written following a trip to the islands, the short piece focuses upon the use of imported contract labour in the form of indentured servants. Used primarily in the sugar industry, the system was, in Coman's view, one of which the results 'advance[d] the interests of the labourers quite as much as those of the planters'. The United States' distaste with such arrangements ended this *status quo* upon annexation, even though the wage system subsequently imposed offered fewer opportunities than before. Covering the decades during which Hawaii underwent massive changes at the hands of Western powers, Coman's work helps illuminate the multiple layers of colonial paternalism in the age of imperialism.

Cambridge University Press has long been a pioneer in the reissuing of out-of-print titles from its own backlist, producing digital reprints of books that are still sought after by scholars and students but could not be reprinted economically using traditional technology. The Cambridge Library Collection extends this activity to a wider range of books which are still of importance to researchers and professionals, either for the source material they contain, or as landmarks in the history of their academic discipline.

Drawing from the world-renowned collections in the Cambridge University Library, and guided by the advice of experts in each subject area, Cambridge University Press is using state-of-the-art scanning machines in its own Printing House to capture the content of each book selected for inclusion. The files are processed to give a consistently clear, crisp image, and the books finished to the high quality standard for which the Press is recognised around the world. The latest print-on-demand technology ensures that the books will remain available indefinitely, and that orders for single or multiple copies can quickly be supplied.

The Cambridge Library Collection will bring back to life books of enduring scholarly value (including out-of-copyright works originally issued by other publishers) across a wide range of disciplines in the humanities and social sciences and in science and technology.

The History of Contract Labor in the Hawaiian Islands

KATHARINE COMAN

CAMBRIDGE
UNIVERSITY PRESS

CAMBRIDGE UNIVERSITY PRESS

Cambridge, New York, Melbourne, Madrid, Cape Town, Singapore,
São Paolo, Delhi, Dubai, Tokyo, Mexico City

Published in the United States of America by Cambridge University Press, New York

www.cambridge.org
Information on this title: www.cambridge.org/9781108020718

© in this compilation Cambridge University Press 2010

This edition first published 1903
This digitally printed version 2010

ISBN 978-1-108-02071-8 Paperback

PUBLICATIONS

OF THE

AMERICAN ECONOMIC ASSOCIATION

THIRD SERIES.   ISSUED QUARTERLY.
VOL. IV, NO. 3.   PRICE, $4.00 PER YEAR.

THE

HISTORY OF CONTRACT LABOR

IN THE

HAWAIIAN ISLANDS

BY

KATHARINE COMAN, PH.B.

AUGUST, 1903

PUBLISHED FOR THE
AMERICAN ECONOMIC ASSOCIATION
BY THE MACMILLAN COMPANY
NEW YORK
LONDON: SWAN SONNENSCHEIN & CO.

PRESS OF
ANDRUS & CHURCH
ITHACA, N. Y.   6687

PREFACE

This study of contract labor is the result of a recent visit to the Hawaiian Islands. In Honolulu, that most hospitable of cities, the author had opportunity to talk with many of the men who have been directly responsible for the laws under which the industrial possibilities of the islands have been developed and who are now engaged, either as planters or as legislators, in devising a substitute labor system. Whatever there may be of value in this monograph is due directly or indirectly to them. I am especially indebted to ex-Attorney General W. O. Smith for access to the early legislation and to court records; to Chief Justice W. F. Frear and Professor W. D. Alexander, who kindly read this essay in manuscript, for some important corrections; to Judge A. S. Hartwell, Mr. L. A. Thurston, and Mr. W. N. Armstrong for many illuminating suggestions; and to Mr. A. P. C. Griffin of the Congressional Library for courteous assistance in hunting down the printed sources of information. The list of references on the subject of contract labor is as yet very brief. The student of this phase of Hawaiian history may therefore congratulate himself on securing the aid of living authorities so wise and so trustworthy.

KATHARINE COMAN.

Cedar Hill, Waltham, Massachusetts,
May 20, 1903.

CONTENTS

CONTRACT LABOR IN THE HAWAIIAN ISLANDS

The problem of converting a tropical country inhabited by a primitive people to the uses of modern industry has been solved in diverse ways by the Spanish in Cuba and the Philippines, by the Dutch in Java and East Sumatra, by the English in British Guiana and the Straits Settlements, by the Belgians in the Congo Free State. In each case zeal for money profit, for the financial success of the enterprise in question, has been moderated and held in check by concern for the well-being of the land and people in process of exploitation. Of these two contending impulses, the industrial is likely to dominate the men immediately concerned in the business enterprise, while the humanitarian comes to the front in the home country, where advantage in the profits derived is but indirect and where wrong done to the nation's honor and prestige is keenly felt.

The experience of the Americans who undertook to civilize the Hawaiian Islands is peculiar in that they enjoyed seventy-five years of immunity from outside interference. The measures determined upon for the development of the country were their own. There was no colonial office to over-rule the local policy. Every candid observer, however, must concede that there was nothing arbitrary in the methods of the missionaries, the white men who were in the long run most influential in directing the course of legislation in the Sandwich Islands. Although the processes of civilization were never gentler or less destructive of native autonomy, the decay of aboriginal society when brought into contact with an advanced social order was no less

inevitable here than in regions where relations between
the aboriginal and the civilized races were less happy.
Within the cycle of a hundred years a primitive agricultural community has been transformed into a highly
specialized industrial system in which every capacity
of land and people is subsidized for the promotion of a
single product.

MODERNIZATION OF NATIVE FEUDALISM.

This primitive organization was closely analogous to
that which we know as feudal.   There was no absolute
title to land ; the right to exploit definite tracts was allowed to the chiefs by the king or over-chief.   The taro
patches were cultivated and all other productive labor
was performed by the common people for the benefit of
the chief on whose land they dwelt.   Like the serfs of
mediæval Europe, the common people rendered service
in products and in labor.   The product service was in
swine, dogs, vegetables, fruit, fish-lines and fish-nets,
calabashes, *kapas*, and the precious red and yellow
feathers from which the cloaks and helmets of state
were manufactured.   Labor service varied with time
and place and gave greater opportunity for extortion.
When the trader's demand for sandal-wood began to ex-
haust the supply, the serfs were forced to penetrate the
dense forests of the mountain tops and bring down
heavy loads on their bare shoulders.   Thousands died
of the unaccustomed cold and fatigue.

The regulation of labor service was one of the first
reforms attempted by the missionaries.   The laws pro-
mulgated by Kamehameha III at Lahaina in 1839
limited and defined the labor tax as follows : " During
the first week of the month, the people are to work two
days for the king and one day for the chief on whose

land they dwell. In the second week of the month, they work one day for the king and two days for the chief. When public work is to be done (the building of roads, bridges, fish-ponds, irrigating-ditches, and the like), the people must work three days in each of the last two weeks of the month until the work be accomplished." Women caring for children were exempt from the labor tax. Money fines were imposed for neglect of service : for each day withheld, fifty cents ; for each half day, twenty-five cents ; for tardiness, twelve and a half cents. These fines were paid to the king or to the chief who suffered the labor loss. On the other hand, the chief who exceeded the labor requirement set by this law must pay a fine to the king and forfeit for six months his claim to the labor of the serfs so overworked. Fines for failure to perform public works were imposed in the same proportion as for private service. A man might exempt himself from all obligation to personal service by the payment of nine dollars per year, four dollars and fifty cents to the king and four dollars and fifty cents to his chief.

With the distribution of lands in 1848,[1] service tenure was abolished and the people were exempted from the labor service due to king and chief. But a public labor tax of twelve days a year was continued ; this might, however, be commuted at fifty cents a day (1850). Thenceforth the taro patches of the chiefs must be cultivated by wage-paid labor. Moreover the presence of

[1] By this memorable act of emancipation Kamehameha III gave the people fee simple title to the lands they were actually cultivating, 28,600 acres, thus creating eleven thousand peasant properties or *kuleanas*. To the chiefs was assigned 1,619,000 acres, and 984,000 acres was reserved as royal demesne. The remaining 1,495,000 acres, mountainous and arid land for the most part, was public property. The arable portions of the public domain were soon after sold to the people at a nominal price.

missionaries and traders created a demand for service
that could be met only by a free labor class. As early
as 1841 a law was published respecting the hire of labor.
" Labor hire as well as other kinds of hire has at the
present time become an extensive business. There are
persons who obtain their whole living and property by
laboring for hire. The law does not condemn that business for it is proper. The law protects it. It would be
a sad thing for the community if the law did not give
protection to him who labors for hire." This law was
enacted by the newly organized legislative body, which,
being composed in the main of the large land owners,
was naturally concerned for the employer's interest. Its
provisions give evidence that the native laborer was not
always worthy of his hire. The labor agreement must
be faithfully performed by both parties. If the laborer
was indolent so that he accomplished little, his wages
might be diminished in proportion to the employer's
loss. If the work was imperfect or was left incomplete
or if the employer should suffer material damage by any
fault of the laborer, the laborer's wages might be diminished or entirely withheld according to the loss sustained.

Another new and extra-feudal demand for labor had
arisen with the advent of the whaling vessels. Whalers
first visited Hawaii in 1820. From that year until
1871, when the business encountered over-whelming
loss in the destruction of the major part of the fleet
in the ice off Cape Belcher, the stout Yankee ships
were accustomed to use the islands as a supply station,
stopping both on the outward and homeward cruise. In
the roadstead between Lahaina and the island of Lanai
as many as one hundred vessels were sometimes
anchored. The whalers came in pursuit not of food
and water only. The Hawaiians were famous sailors,

and it was customary to take on a crew of brawny kanakas for service in the north seas. By 1846 it was thought advisable to regulate this employment. The act authorizing the enlistment of native sailors provided that application for permission to enlist natives on a foreign vessel must be made to the governor of the island to which they belonged, and that shipping articles must be deposited with him stating the name and nationality of the vessel and the destination, object, and term of service proposed. The master of the vessel must further execute a bond to the amount of one hundred dollars for each man so enlisted as surety for the payment of his personal taxes and for the just fulfilment of the contract. The sailor on his part could give no bond, but the authorities were made responsible for him. " The governors shall have power, after the provisions of the preceding articles are fully complied with, to compel the embarkation of any subjects of these Islands so voluntarily enlisted by a foreign captain, and for that purpose, in case of desertion, he may cause them to be arrested and conveyed on board." [1]

Still another labor demand, destined to be far greater and more permanent, developed with the systematic cultivation of sugar. Sugar cane grew luxuriantly on the islands, and a low grade sugar had been manufactured as early as 1823, the cane being crushed between wooden rollers and the juice boiled down in open kettles; but the cultivation of the cane on plantation scale was not undertaken until 1835. In this year a mill was erected at Koloa on Kauai, and the industry was fairly inaugurated. By 1838 twenty-two mills were in operation, the windward side of Hawaii and Maui proving to be as well adapted as Kauai to the culture of

[1] Section VI, law of 1846.

the cane. It was soon demonstrated that the islands afford almost ideal conditions for the growing of sugar—fertile soil, abundant rainfall, and a climate so equable that the cane can be brought to full maturity and the highest percentage of saccharine matter developed. These natural advantages guarantee the Hawaiian sugar planter to-day a yield three or four times as great as that of Cuba or Louisiana. Disadvantages quite as permanent and inevitable are the distance from the world markets and the scarcity of labor.[1]

THE LABOR PROBLEM.

The scarcity of labor began to be recognized as a serious handicap to the industrial development of the islands as early as 1850. A law of that year recites: "Whereas, the native population is diminishing" and the "want of labor is severely felt by planters and other agriculturists, the price of provisions being thereby enhanced," and "whereas many natives have emigrated to California and there died in great misery, be it enacted that no native subject of the king may leave these islands without express permission given on proved necessity." The planters soon discovered that the cultivation of sugar on a profitable scale required a very considerable land area and an abundant supply of low grade labor. Every subsequent improvement in the industry, every new application of machinery, has emphasized this dual necessity. Steam-plows, irrigation from pumping stations, hauling of the cane by rail, enhanced capacity of the mill—each effort to reduce cost of production involves an increased

[1] According to W. C. Stubbs, director of the Louisiana agricultural experiment station, the Louisiana average is one and one-half tons of sugar per acre, the Cuban from one to two tons, while the plantations of Hawaii boast an average yield of five tons ; but in Hawaii it takes from three to six months longer to mature the crop.

expenditure by way of fixed capital that is justified only by proportionate increase of the area to be cultivated. Moreover the vicissitudes of a sugar crop require that masses of labor be brought to bear without delay at the given time and place. Cane must be cut when it is ripe or the stalks grow dry and woody. Once cut, the cane must be got to the mill within three days or it sours and is unfit for use. Thousands of dollars may be lost by a delay of a few hours.

By 1850 it was becoming painfully evident that the native population would be quite inadequate to meet this labor demand. The Hawaiians were disinclined to the steady, monotonous labor required in the cane-fields; and, moreover, the race was dying out with startling rapidity. Captain Cook's estimate of the population of the islands in 1779 was 400,000. He was probably deceived by the crowds of people who came to the coasts to see the marvelous visitors, the fire-breathing gods. A more conservative estimate rates the population in the discovery epoch at 300,000. The missionaries in 1823 reckoned the population at 142,000. The first census, taken in 1832, enumerated 130,313. A second census taken four years later, returned but 108,579. A third census, taken in 1850, gave the native population 84,165 and the foreign 1962. The native race has continued to decline in numbers, the census of 1900 enumerating but 29,799 Hawaiians and 7857 part Hawaiians in a total population of 154,000.

LEGALIZATION OF CONTRACT LABOR.

The year 1850 marks the initiation of a systematic effort to meet the labor demand of the planters. In that year the legislative assembly legalized two forms of labor contract hitherto unknown to these islands, [1] apprenticeship and indentured service. The Act for the Government of Masters and Servants, so far as it concerned apprenticeship, closely resembles that of Massachusetts. It provides that minors may be bound out as apprentices or servants by father, mother, or guardian, or by the governor of the island—boys from ten to twenty years, girls from ten to eighteen years. The contract, which must be signed by both parties, binds the master to teach reading, writing, and, in case of a male, arithmetic, and requires that the recompense to be rendered to the minor at the end of the term be plainly stated. Charges of cruelty or misusage may be brought against the master by the parents, guardian, or governor, or by the apprentice himself after expiration of his term. In case such a suit is sustained, the apprentice is discharged and the damages recovered become the property of said minor. In case an apprentice departs from service, the justice on complaint of the master shall issue a warrant for his apprehension. The captured apprentice must be returned to his master and is bound to render additional service for double the time of his absence, provided such service does not exceed the year immediately following the original term. The same act provides that a person more than twenty years of age may contract himself to service for a term not exceeding five years. If a laborer so bound wilfully absents himself from service he may be apprehended, restored to his master, and bound to additional service for double the time of absence. If he refuses to serve,

---

[1] By the Organic Act of 1846 the minister of the interior was authorized to sieze vagrants and to apprentice them out for a term of not more than one year ; two-thirds of the wages were to be paid the va_ grant and one-third was to go to the goverment. The master was permitted to use coercive force if the vagrant refused to work.

he may be committed to prison and confined at hard labor until he will consent to serve according to contract. A second desertion may be punished by three months at hard labor for the state, in addition to the service due his master.[1] If the master, on the other hand, has been convicted of cruelty, misusage, or violation of contract, he may be fined from five dollars to one hundred dollars, and, in default of payment, be confined at hard labor until the same is paid.

The legislation declaring the terms under which an adult might contract his services for a term of years was an adaptation of the American shipping law. It was probably suggested by the practice of taking service on the whaling ships above alluded to ; indeed, engaging for service on a plantation is still termed "shipping" in Hawaii. The analogy with the terms of indentured service in the American colonies is also evident. The bond servant of colonial Virginia, whether working out a penal sentence or making good the cost of his passage, was equally under obligation to serve to the end of his term. An attempt to escape was sharply dealt with. The sheriff summoned the men of the hundred to follow with hue and cry, and the runaway, if captured, was compelled to serve an additional term of double the time of his absence.[2]

---

[1] Amendment of 1860.

[2] " Whereas there are divers loitering runaways, who very often absent themselves from their masters service and sometimes in a long time cannot be found, the loss of their time and the charge of the seeking them, often exceeding the value of their labor : Be it therefore enacted That all runaways shall be liable to make satisfaction by service, after the times by custom or indenture are expired, viz. double their time of service so neglected; and if the time of their Running away was in the Crop, and the charge of recovering them extraordinary, the Court shall adjudg a longer time of service, proportionable to the damage the master shall make appear he hath sustained." Collection of the laws of Virginia, 1662, chap. 102.

That in the thought of the legislators of 1850 the laborer contemplated by the Master and Servants Act was the kanaka is made evident in an amendment of 1868, providing that the contract must be printed in both English and Hawaiian. A legal form was provided, with blanks for inserting the names of parties to the contract, the place, the terms, and the wages agreed upon.[1] Hawaiians continued to be employed on the sugar plantations, though in ever decreasing numbers. The number working under labor contracts was 1319 in 1886, 399 in 1896, and 163 in 1899.[2] A writer in the Hawaiian Annual of 1895 declares that "For all round plantation work no imported unskilled laborers have proved their [the kanakas'] equal;" but the natives who must work for their living prefer to do so as teamsters and cow-boys or as sailors. Field labor is not to their mind.

The impossibility of supplying the plantations with native labor was clearly forseen in 1850, and a section was incorporated in the Master and Servants Act to the effect that "all engagements of service contracted in a foreign country to be executed in this" are valid except that "engagements made for a longer period than ten years be reduced to that limit." This is the legal basis of the contract labor system of the Hawaiian Islands.

---

[1] A specimen contract : By this indenture the owners of Hana Plantation, Island of Maui, of the first part, agree with Kealaula of the second part as follows : 1. I, Kealaula, agree to work faithfully and diligently for said owners of Hana Plantation for the term of eighteen months, from the first day of September, 1874, (each month to consist of 26 days labor) in their service and at such place as they or their agents may assign me to work, not less than ten hours work per day. 2. The owners of Hana Plantation aforesaid agree faithfully to pay to Kealaula the sum of eight dollars ($8.) for each month of faithful service to the end of the term specified above, and also to provide him with poi, not with meat, until this agreement expires.

[2] See table B, p. 64.

Under this law, in force from 1850 to 1897, one hundred
and fifteen thousand laborers were imported into the
Hawaiian Islands, and the resources of the country have
been developed to a degree that would have been quite
impossible had the planters been restricted to native
labor or to voluntary immigration. The history of this
labor system, of the attempts made to regulate and control it and to maintain American institutions alongside
of it, constitutes a most interesting phase of industrial
experience.

CHINESE COOLIES.

The Royal Hawaiian Agricultural Society was
founded in 1850 with a view to promoting the interests
of the planters along various lines. The labor problem,
being to the fore, naturally engaged the first energies of
the association. The prospectus sets forth that " The
introduction of coolie labor from China to supply the
places of the rapidly decreasing native population, is a
question that is already agitated among us, and should
such a step become necessary, the aid of such an association in accomplishing this object would become
of great benefit." Two years later the society engaged Captain Cass of the bark *Thetis* to bring in
Chinese laborers under contract as provided for by
the Master and Servants Act. The one hundred and
eighty coolies imported in 1852 were bound to serve
for a term of five years at three dollars per month in
addition to passage prepaid and food, clothing, and
shelter provided by the planter who had engaged their
services. The cost of transportation was fifty dollars
per man, and maintenance per man was estimated at
five dollars per month. The cost of the labor may
therefore be reckoned at about nine dollars a month.

Later in this same year Captain Cass brought in one hundred more Chinese coolies. The experiment was highly satisfactory, and the president of the society in his annual report congratulated the country on securing such "quiet, able, and willing men."

The satisfaction of the laborers was no less, if we may judge from a statement published in the *Chinese Mail*: "The coolies shipped for South America are hired laborers, and according to some accounts, virtually slaves; but we are told that it is otherwise with those sent to the Sandwich Islands. Fortunately that traffic was undertaken by a man of much humanity and good sense; and according to the account that we have received from one who speaks from actual observation, but who has no connection with or interest in the adventures, Captain Cass entered into engagement with the planters of the Sandwich Islands to import Chinese laborers for the sugar plantations,—the planters binding themselves to pay the laborers four dollars a month from the time of their arrival; while cooks, house-servants, and gardeners have been engaged at salaries as high as sixteen dollars,—and as the wages are not promised merely, but paid, and the coolies are well treated, they are not only contented, but have urged their friends at home to join them."

POLYNESIANS.

The importation of aliens was naturally regarded with jealousy by the Hawaiians. In 1852 Kamehameha III undertook to transport the whole population of Pitcairn's Island to the royal estates, hoping thus to secure tenants and cultivators closely allied to the native race in blood and language. This project failed because the English consul refused to allow the deportation of these islanders unless they came as British subjects. Since this might jeopardize the newly won and much prized independence of the islands, the scheme was abandoned. Kamehameha IV repeatedly urged the importation of Polynesians with a view to recruiting the native stock. There was a strong sentiment in favor of providing, not labor for the planters merely, but men and women of vigorous physique who would marry with the Hawaiians and so replenish the deserted fields. But the prime concern of the planters was to grow sugar-cane. They did not wish to be burdened with women and children. Moreover, it was by no means clear that natives of the South Sea islands were any more inclined to monotonous field labor than were the Hawaiians.[1]

The hope of reinvigorating the native stock was not abandoned, however. The fifth Kamehameha came under the influence of a man who, first and last, had much to say concerning the labor problem in the Hawaiian Islands. Walter Murray Gibson, an adventurer of dubious precedents, acquired large estates on the island of Lanai and there conducted a series of immigration experiments. To his mind the problem was primarily a population problem. A permanent labor supply could only be provided by importing a people vigorous and prolific and thus repleting the energies of the exhausted Hawaiian race. Gibson strenuously urged the introduction of Polynesians under the patronage of the state. In 1864 the legislature voted an appropriation of $36,000 for the transplanting of a considerable number of Polynesians of both sexes. " For their support and employment " the immigrants were to

---

[1] The first actual experiment was made in 1859 when ten South Sea Islanders were brought over and placed on Koloa plantation as contract laborers.

be bound to service for a given term. The law declared that all such contracts should provide, as far as
might be, that the employers should receive as many
women as men, and that suitable provision should be
made for the support of such women. In 1869 the
Mauna Loa was sent to the Caroline Islands for the first
shipment of Polynesians under government auspices.
She brought back eighty men, women, and children,
and these were hired out to planters on the island of
Oahu, since the government desired to have the experiment under immediate observation. The men were to
be paid four dollars per month and the women three
dollars in addition to food, clothing, and shelter, and the
planter was to pay thirty dollars toward the passage
money of each Polynesian in his employ. In a second
expedition the *Mauna Loa* secured forty-two men and
women from Danger Islands. They were contracted for
at a slightly advanced wage ; men four dollars and fifty
cents, women three dollars and fifty cents.

This altogether praise-worthy undertaking suffered
the fate of many another optimistic attempt to improve
on the natural order of things. It was denounced as
man-stealing, or in facetious phrase " black-birding."
In its issue of March 12, 1869, the *New York Tribune*
announced : " The coolie trade in the Sandwich Islands
has, for sometime past, taken on a development which
leaves but little difference between it and the slave
trade. It is especially the natives of the small Polynesian Islands who are imported, often entirely against
their will, and compelled to work." There is no evidence of any complaint of ill-treatment on the part
of these people, but they sickened in the strange environ-
ment. They proved quite unsatisfactory as laborers,
moreover, and were, in accordance with the agreements

made with them, returned to their homes at the expense of the government. The men who were instrumental in forwarding this immigration scheme should not be judged by rumor as to what was done or left undone on those hazardous cruises in the South Seas, but by their own statements. To the recruiting agent in the South Sea islands the president of the Board of Immigration wrote: "The point upon which I insist is that our honor and good name must be protected, that no means of any kind in any way disreputable be used in obtaining these people." And again, "I make this a condition that you do not trade in rum, guns, or ammunition while gathering these people for us." Captain Jackson of the *Stormbird*, who was sent to Rotumah in 1878, was instructed to "use all fair and just means to induce these people to emigrate to these Islands, and bear in mind we are anxious to have women and children as well as men."

Private recruiting for South Sea islanders was later allowed, but only on condition that the immigrants should be under control of the Board of Immigration and that the following instructions be observed by shipmasters : " 1. Vessels must be fitted out with all comforts and supplied with food, water, and medicines sufficient for the number of people that the laws of the Kingdom allow them to carry, and no liquor, guns, or ammunition shall be taken for purposes of trade. 2. All acts in procuring labor shall be honest and above reproach and no deception of any kind used. They shall thoroughly interpret and fully explain to all the people what is expected of them, as well as the kind of labor, pay, and food. 3. To make contracts for not less than three years at five dollars, six dollars, and seven dollars a month for the first, second, and third year respectively, and for women four dollars, five dollars, and six dollars along with food, house, and bed-clothing. Their taxes to be paid by their employers and their wages payable in cash at the end of each month. If they so desire they shall be returned to their homes at the expiration of their contract. 4. To bring as many women as men and the children belonging to the families. To make no contracts with children, and those under fourteen years to go to school free of expense. No work to be done on Sunday and no master to strike a servant." In 1880 Rev. H. Bingham[1] was appointed special inspector for the South Sea islanders. His duties were defined as follows : " To make tours on the several islands of the group where there are South Sea islanders employed, to inspect their general treatment and condition, to report when necessary any violation of the laws, the regulations of the Board or the conditions under which they were engaged, to inspect the quarters, food, and arrangements for medical care and enquire into any complaints that they may have to make, explaining to them their rights and their duties and helping them by advice to obtain redress in case of wrong ; to see that their children are given the facilities for education in district schools, and report to the Board such modification of contracts or other arrangements as might to him appear to conduce to the well-being of the people, as also all statistics that he may gather."

STATE REGULATION.

It was the desire to promote imigration, while avoiding the evils of the coolie trade, that suggested the

---

[1] Mr. Bingham had labored as a missionary for ten years among the Gilbert Islanders, had reduced their language to writing, and translated the Bible and several other books into Gilbertese.

Bureau of Immigration. Kamehameha V. said in an address from the throne in 1867 : " Our agricultural enterprises have been urged forward with such energy on every island of the group as to render the importation of laborers necessary. I am of the opinion that the Goverment is the proper agent to carry out such a measure, and that means ought to be placed at its disposal to undertake it promptly. The wants of our agriculture, the dictates of humanity, and the preservation of our race demand that the government should control this action." In accordance with the King's recommendation, a committee of the Privy Council was constituted the Board of Immigration and instructed to submit " such measures as may be necessary to secure the importation of a sufficient number of foreign laborers to supply the wants of planters and others" and to devise " such regulations as may be deemed expedient, touching the contracts to be made with such laborers, as well as the terms and conditions upon which they are to be assigned after their arrival in this kingdom." The recommendations of the board when approved by the Privy Council were to have the force of laws.

The principle of state regulation once established, an agitation was set on foot for the reform of the labor system, and various amendments to the Master and Servants Act were proposed. In 1872 the reform element secured a majority vote in the legislature, and a thorough revision of the terms of the labor contract resulted. For the protection of parties to contracts authorized by section 1417 of the civil code, a law was passed providing that every contract for service must be acknowledged by both master and servant before an authorized officer of the government. The certificate of acknowledgement should state that after the contract

had been read and explained to the parties, "they sever-
ally acknowledged that they understood the same and
that they had executed the same voluntarily." An
agent or recorder for each district was provided who
was directed to cause money advanced to the servant
to be paid in his presence and to keep an accurate record
of contracts acknowledged before him, "which record
shall set forth the names and residence of the parties,
the date and term of the contract, the amount of advance paid and the wages stipulated for."

The distinction between contract labor and serf labor
had never been ignored. The laborer was not bound to
the plantation. The contract established a personal bond
and ceased to be operative on the death of the master
or in case the plantation changed hands. This principle was several times affirmed by decisions of the Supreme Court.[1] Transfers of contract from one employer
to another were not permitted until the convention with
Japan (1886). Such transfers, in the case of Japanese laborers and of Chinese under the restrictive law of 1892,
were allowed only with the consent of the employer and
laborer concerned and with the approval of the Board
of Immigration. A laborer might commute any por-
tion of his term of service by making over to his employer the just proportion of the sum advanced for his
transportation expenses. The extension of the term of
service was now guarded against abuse. "No contract
laborer may be compelled to work beyond the term of his
contract in liquidation of a debt entered into during such
term." Any contract stipulations to this effect were de-

[1] 1887. J. Nott vs. Kanahele. "This is a personal contract and the
laborer is not bound to the land as a serf."

1889. C. Afong vs. Kale. An application for release from contract
on the ground that the laborer had been made to work on a schooner
instead of on a sugar plantation was not allowed.

clared void. " In all cases when any person under contract to serve another shall be sentenced by any court to
make to his master satisfaction for loss of time by desertion by working for a period of time beyond that contracted for, he shall be paid his wages for such extra time
worked at the rate stipulated for in the contract." By
an amendment of 1882, the extension of the labor term
as punishment for desertion was prohibited. The recovered servant might be compelled to serve to the end
of his original term and no more. A contract laborer
escaping from service might be fined five dollars for the
first offense and ten dollars for each subsequent offense,
and in default of payment should be confined at hard
labor until fine and costs were paid. When he had met
the prescribed penalty he was to be restored to his master to serve for the remainder of his original term.

In case of ill-usage the servant might secure redress
from the courts as under the laws of colonial Virginia.[1]
" If any master shall be guilty of any cruelty, misusage
or violation of any of the terms of the contract, toward

[1] " Whereas the Barbarous usage of some Servants by cruel Masters,
brings so much Scandal and Infamy to the Country in general, that people who would willingly adventure themselves hither, are through fear
thereof diverted, and by that means the supplies of particular men, and
the well seating of his Majestie's Country very much obstructed : Be it
therefore enacted, That every Master shall provide for his Servants competent Diet, Clothing and Lodging, and that he shall not exceed the
bounds of moderation, in correcting them beyond the merit of their
offenses ; and that it shall be lawful for any Servant, giving notice to
their Masters, having just cause of complaint against them, for harsh
and bad usage, or else for want of Diet and convenient Necessaries ; to
repair to the next Commissioner to make his or their Complaint ; and
if the said Commissioner shall find by just proof that the said Servants'
cause of Complaint is just, the said Commissioner is hereby required to
give order for the Warning of such Master to the next County Court,
where the matter in difference shall be determined, and the Servant
have remedy for his grievance." Collection of the laws of Virginia,
1662, Chap. 103.

3

any person bound to service under the 1417th or 1418th sections (of the Civil Code), such person may make complaint to any District or Police Justice, who shall summon the parties before him, examine into, hear and determine the complaint and in all such examinations the complainant shall be a competent witness; and if the complaint shall be sustained, such person shall be discharged from all obligations of service and the master shall be fined in a sum not less than $5, nor more than $100, and in default of the payment thereof be imprisoned at hard labor till the sum is paid." [1]

A law of 1876 prescribed that in all contracts where the length of a day's labor was not specified, nine hours should constitute a working day. The laborer was entitled to extra compensation for work in excess of such time. A law of 1884 further guarded the laborer's interests: " Whereas laborers serving under written contracts are sometimes oppressed through having their wages excessively reduced for lost time, every laborer serving under written contract shall be entitled to his full pay under the contract, according to the time he has worked, and no master shall deduct from the wages of any such laborer for lost time, more than the amount of money representing such lost time."

A law of 1880 fixed a sanitary standard for plantation " camps." A tenement for contract laborers must be built eighteen inches from the ground, must have a water-tight roof, and must provide three hundred cubic feet of air space for each adult lodger and three hundred for every two children; the house must be kept in good

[1] Ruling of the Supreme Court, 1853. The King vs. *in re* Greenwell : " The whipping of servants or laborers is not justifiable under the laws of this Kingdom. A master may correct his apprentice with due moderation."

repair and white-washed frequently; the yard must be well-drained and free from rubbish; a cess-pool must be provided for every six adults. The penalty for non-compliance with any one of these requirements was fifty dollars. The officers of the board of health were to have free access to the laborers' quarters.

The Board of Immigration had full power to direct the course of immigration and to determine from what source the "foreign laborers" should be derived. By the king's ordinance of 1865, private persons were prohibited from introducing bound laborers into the kingdom without the express license of the Board of Immigration.[1] Heavy penalties were imposed for evasion of this prohibition. Planters were fined $800 and ship-masters $100 for each offense.

The immigration system so regulated compares favorably with the coolie trade in its best estate as practised in British Guiana under the Consolidated Immigration Ordinances of 1864 and 1891. The work of the Bureau of Immigration in prescribing the number of laborers to be imported, the countries from which they might be drawn, the vessels in which they might be carried, the accommodations that must be afforded them at sea and in port, the terms of the contracts to be made with them, and the living and working conditions on the plantations to which they were assigned, is closely analogous to that of the immigration agent general of British Guiana and his staff of deputies, clerks, and physicians. The Bureau of Immigration sent inspectors on a circuit of the planta-

---

[1] A law of 1894 reënacted in 1897 declared contracts made with laborers antecedent to their arrival in Hawaii null and void "unless such contracts shall have received the written approval of the Board of Immigration."

tions four times a year to make sure that the laborers' dwellings were kept up to the required sanitary standard and that sufficient medical care was provided. The inspectors were further empowered to investigate all complaints, to settle disputes wherever possible, and to arrange for commutations and transfers of service. Biennial reports were made to the legislative assembly (printed 1882-1899) in which the policy of the Board was set forth and recommendations for improving upon the immigration system submitted. After 1886 a detailed report on the sixty odd plantations was incorporated, stating the number and nationality of laborers and the sanitary conditions for each, and reporting breaches of the law, maltreatment of laborers, etc. [1] It is worthy of remark that the provisions for the well-being of the laborer which were imposed upon the planters and the government of Guiana by parliament and the colonial office were adopted by a representative legislature in Hawaii in the interest of the public good.

There are three points of advantage in favor of the Indian coolie. First, the system of recruiting in India is under the supervision of the protector of immigrants in Calcutta. The Bureau of Immigration maintained an authorized recruiting agent at Madeira, at Hongkong, and at Yokohama and specified the vessels and steamship lines by which immigrants might be transported. It could not in the nature of things go further. Second, the wages of the laborers transported to British Guiana were not fixed in advance, and the indenture when made out at Georgetown bound the coolie to serve a

---

[1] *E. g.*, in the report for 1897, there is an account of a riot which had occurred on Lihue plantation, Kauai. The inspector investigated, the head *luna* was discharged, and the manager reprimanded and told that he would be held to strict account for the better treatment of his laborers in future.

given master for five years without stipulated wages. The law provided that the remuneration of the coolie might not be less than that of the free laborer and that the task assigned him might not be heavier. The practice of leaving the compensation of the imported laborer to be determined by the conditions of the free labor market threw upon him the responsibility of determining his wage-rate—a responsibility to which he, a stranger and a bondsman, was hardly adequate. The legal minimum was fixed at a shilling a day for five days work a week. The average earnings of a good workman were estimated at two shillings. The earnings of the Portuguese contract laborer who in 1877 was guaranteed by the Board of Immigration[1] ten dollars a month with fuel, lodging, and food were considerably better. Third, the Hindoo coolie who, at the end of his five years, reindentured for a second five year term was given a bounty of fifty dollars, amounting to the cost of return passage. The laborer was more valuable in his second term than in the first because he had become thoroughly acclimatized, familiar with plantation life, and a skilled workman. The Hawaiian government offered no such inducement, but the laborers not unfrequently reëngaged for a second and even a third term, steady employment at advanced wages proving a sufficient inducement. Experienced laborers, whether free or under contract, commanded higher wages.

In the report of 1888–1890 the Board of Immigration estimated plantation wages as follows :—

	Contract Laborers	Free Laborers
Hawaiian	$18.58 per month.	$20.64 per month.
Portuguese	19.53 "	22.25 "
Japanese	15.58 "	18.84 "
Chinese	17.61 "	17.47 "
South Sea Islander	15.81 "	18.56 "

[1] Edward Jenkins, The Coolie, his rights and wrongs. 1871.

The figures show a higher average wage in case of the free laborer, but the majority of contract laborers were serving for the first term or were inferior men who could find employment only under contract and at low wages.

EXPERIMENTS OF THE BOARD OF IMMIGRATION.

Any impartial study of the proceedings of the Board will disclose a persistent and sustained effort to secure immigrants who would be desirable not only as laborers but as citizens. The initial attempt to bring in natives of the South Sea islands, men and women, has already been recited. The hope of thus renewing the aboriginal race was not abandoned, though the people thus introduced were for the most part discouraging material both as laborers and as citizens. As late as 1883 a shipment of thirty South Sea islanders is recorded. In the twenty years from 1865 to 1885, 2448 Polynesians were brought into the Hawaiian Islands. A bare six hundred remain, only forty-six being plantation laborers. Plans were early set on foot for inducing free immigration from the Azores, the Canary, and the Cape Verde Islands. The impoverished state of these Portuguese settlements, after the failure of their vineyards, gave reason to hope that the superfluous population might be drawn to a land where demand for labor was in excess of supply ; but it soon became evident that the Portuguese would not undertake the long journey to an unknown country without artificial stimulus. Reverting to the Orient, the Board in 1865 commissioned Dr. Hillebrand, a man of scientific attainments,[1] to make a tour of China, Japan, Malaysia, and India with a view to studying the labor possibilities of these over-populated regions and

[1] Author of The Flora of the Hawaiian Islands.

making recommendations that might serve as a basis for a systematic scheme of immigration.

But the theories and aspirations of the Board and of such doctrinaires as Gibson were continually held in check by the incessant demand of the planters for an immediate supply of laborers. Again and again the exigencies of the sugar crop proved a more potent argument than any hypothesis as to the ultimate good of the state. The immediate necessity could best be met by the importation of Chinese coolies. The immigration table, [pp. 63,] shows conclusively that the stream of Chinese immigration received no perceptible check from the establishment of the Board. Ten years earlier Prince Liholiho, in an address before the Hawaiian Agricultural Society, had put the matter in a nut-shell: " Chinese have been introduced here, and more are on their way hither.[1] With all their faults and a considerable disposition to hang themselves, they have been found very useful. Suffice it to say that some of our largest sugar and coffee plantations are now chiefly dependent upon them for the principal amount of labor done. That they might be better than they are ought not to be used as an argument against them. That they are procurable, that they have been procured, that their wages are reasonable, that you can calculate on retaining them for a certain term, that the climate suits them and that they are handy in the house and in the fields are great facts. Excepting what relates to these coolies, all that bears upon the subject of imported labor, is just theory and speculation."

Forced to fall back upon China, the Board of Immigration directed its attention to improving the conditions

[1] Seven hundred Chinese coolies were brought into the Hawaiian Islands between 1852 and 1864.

of the coolie trade and to securing a class of immigrants that might prove less harmful to the social interests of the islands. Dr. Hillebrand's first step was to arrange for the transportation of five hundred Chinese laborers. Reliable recruiting agents were selected, and Rev. Mr. Lobscheid, formerly a missionary in Hongkong, was made responsible for the physical well-being of the immigrants. Twenty-five per cent of the people were to be women, and they were shipped in two commodious vessels as a precaution against disease.[1] The horrors of the coolie trade as carried on by the Portuguese at Macao called forth a vigorous denunciation from the good Doctor.

The Chinese were entirely satisfactory as laborers, but they were regarded with little favor by the Hawaiians and by the artisan class who did not look upon the sugar industry as the corner-stone of the state. Their vigorous protests induced the Board to try another experiment. Negotiations were opened through the Hawaiian counsul in Japan for the introduction of

[1] The cost of importing one of these laborers was as follows:—

Recruiting, lodging in Hongkong, two suits clothes, provision for voyage	$25
Passage money	12
Commission	4
Board expenses	10
Bonus paid to men	8
Bonus paid to women	20

The expenses of transportation ($59) were met by the planter who engaged the laborer's services, but all except the bonus and the Board expenses were treated as an advance and deducted from wages month by month. Thus the final cost of this labor was less than that of the Chinese first imported, but even so there was no difficulty in securing men. With wages at $4 per month and $2 as a New Year's gift, the coolie earned in three years $150 in addition to the bonus of $8. After having made good the advance payment ($41) he would have received $119. Since all living expenses, food, shelter, fuel, and clothing were provided him, the bulk of this sum was clear gain.

laborers from that kingdom. The Japanese government furthered the project, and in 1868 one hundred
and forty-eight immigrants were secured. They were
under contract for three years' service at four dollars
per month for men and three dollars per month for
women. Two Japanese head-men were provided for
each gang of twenty-five laborers, and were paid one
dollar per month additional. A head-man for the whole
company was paid $150 a year, with living expenses,
for his services as interpreter and mediator. All complaints were to be laid before the Board and there adju-
dicated. The system of fines for minor offenses, in
vogue on some plantations, was abolished so far as these
laborers were concerned. All costs of transportation
were met by the employers, and food, lodging, and
medicine were to be provided free. The experiment
might have been a permanent success but for misunder-
standings due to the ignorance of the interpreters. The
Japanese government, becoming alarmed for the safety
of the people, sent a commission of inquiry to Hawaii.
The commissioners reported, " We have everywhere
found our countrymen well cared for and kindly treated
by their employers." Notwithstanding, the Japanese
authorities refused, for the time being, to consider any
further propositions for immigration under labor contract.

THE PORTUGUESE.

The reformed immigration system was hardly in full
operation when the Reciprocity Treaty with the United
States gave a marked stimulus to sugar culture [1] and
produced an even more insistent demand for labor. To
meet this emergency, the Board commissioned Dr. Hillebrand, then residing in the Azores, to arrange for the

[1] See Table C, p. 65.

transportation of Portuguese laborers. The terms offered in the contracts of 1877 were most generous.[1]
Passage money was to be prepaid and refunded to the
planter only in case the laborer withdrew from his contract before the expiration of the three years' term, and
then in proportion to the amount of service unperformed.
Employment was guaranteed by the Board at the rate
of $10 for men, $6 to $8 for women, with food, lodging,
and medical attendance provided. A day's ration was
to consist of one pound of beef or one-half pound of fish,
fresh or salt as might be best obtained, one and one-half
pounds of rice, one-half pound of taro or other vegeta-
ble, one-third ounce of tea. Garden ground was to be

[1] Labor contract of 1885 : "This agreement, entered into between
Augusto da Silva Moreira and Hoffnung, agent of the Board of Immigration, Witnesseth :—That whereas the party of the second part is
desirous of emigrating to the Hawaiian Islands, there to be employed
as an agricultural laborer, under the direction of the Board of Immigration : Now, therefore, in consideration of a passage to the Hawaiian
Islands on board the steamship *Hansa* and a further undertaking by
the party of the first part that the said Board of Immigration will pay
or cause to be paid, to the party of the second part, wages at the rate
of $9 per month, with board and lodging for himself and children un-
der twelve years of age, for each and every month of 26 days' service
faithfully performed during the existence of this agreement (a day's
service to be ten hours in the field and twelve hours in the sugar-house) ;
such wages to be paid at the end of each calendar month, reckoning
from the date of the commencement of such service after arrival at
Honolulu,—and in consideration of a further undertaking on the part
of the party of the first part to secure the party of the second part full
protection under the Hawaiian law, as fully as the same is enjoyed by
the native born subjects of the kingdom, and likewise in case of sickness that he shall be supplied with proper medical attendance and that
the said children shall be properly instructed in the native schools,
the said party of the second part will duly and faithfully perform such
lawful and proper labor as he may be directed to perform under the
auspices of the said Board of Immigration for the term of three years,
counting from the day on which he shall commence such service after
arrival in the kingdom of Hawaii, it being always understood that the
contracted party shall not work on Sundays or on any holiday recognized by the government, and that his services shall not be transferred
without his consent."

supplied in immediate connection with the house.   These
were much better terms than had been accorded any previous laborers, but the greater cost was made good by the
superior efficiency of Europeans.   Recruiting agents in
the Azores were thus instructed by the Board :   " We
are particularly desirous that no underhand or unjust
means of any kind be used in inducing these people to
emigrate.   All that come shall be well used.   Every
promise made in the contracts shall be faithfully carried
out."   The Board made good its assurances by promptly
investigating complaints as to insufficient food and
medical attendance on ship-board.   It was made evident
that there was no more sickness among the passengers
than was inevitable on the long voyage round the
Horn.

The arrival of the first Portuguese was an event of
critical importance to the industrial and social future of
the islands.   There were eighty men, forty women, and
sixty children.   The Portuguese consul at Honoluln,
Mr. Perry, supervised the signing of their contracts,
allowing them full liberty to choose their employers.
In accordance with the instructions of the board, families were not separated in the assignment of laborers.
The planters expressed themselves so well content
with this experiment that steps were taken to place
Portuguese immigration on a permanent basis.   Mr.
Hutcheson was appointed Hawaiian consul at Maderia
with a view to facilitating the recruiting of immigrants,
while Hoffnung and Company, ship-masters of London,
were commissioned to transport from one thousand to ten
thousand people at ninety dollars per capita.   The cost
of transportation was to be refunded by the men.   Half
the passage of women and the entire passage of children
would be met by the Board.   The proportion of women

was to be from thirty-five to forty per cent. Children were allowed at the rate of two to a family. The announcement that twelve hundred Portuguese were on the way to the islands gave general satisfaction. Comic, therefore, was the dismay of the Board when the *Ravenscrag* arrived with one hundred and thirty-three men, one hundred and ten women, and one hundred and seventy-six children. Later shipments were even more unprofitable from the planters' point of view. The Portuguese persisted in bringing their families, male and female, young and old, till the Board was forced to make a new arrangement. The planter's share of the cost of transporting the women was to be paid in monthly deductions from the wages of the men and women concerned. Children from twelve to thirteen years might be contracted to labor at four dollars per month, children from thirteen to fourteen years at five dollars, from fourteen to fifteen years at six dollars per month.[1] Passage money for children under twelve years was still to be met by the Board. The heavy expenditures of the government on this account could only be made good in the course of years when these unwelcome children became tax-paying citizens.

From the beginning the governor of Madeira had caused trouble about the labor contracts, sometimes annulling them outright so that the men arrived under no further obligation than to repay the cost of their transportation, an obligation easily shirked. In 1881 H. A. P. Carter was sent to Lisbon as Minister Plenipotentiary for the purpose of placing the emigration of laborers from the Western Islands to Hawaii on a treaty basis. He succeeded in negotiating a convention between Portugal and the Hawaiian Islands in which it

[1] See Table B, p. 64.

was agreed: 1. that contracts for service were to be binding on both parties; 2. that adequate protection was to be afforded the immigrants under the Hawaiian law; 3. that immigrant ships should conform to specified requirements in regard to space, quantity and quality of food, medicine, sanitation, etc.

The arrivals of the next three years amounted to seven thousand seven hundred, yet the laborers commanded better and better wages. In 1884 the Board was constrained to offer sixteen dollars a month with lodging and fuel but without food, with the further promise of an allowance of two dollars a month for one child and four dollars for two or more. This unlooked for surrender of a long contested point was occasioned by the dread signs of exhaustion in this much prized labor supply. In 1884 Hoffnung wrote: " Our agent at St. Michaels finds it less easy to recruit emigrants from that island from which we have already taken some six thousand or seven thousand souls. He informs us that all wages have recently been doubled and there are other signs that the surplus population has been disposed of. Moreover the Brazilian and other governments are now offering special inducements to emigrants for their respective countries, and the competition is carrying off a good many to other fields of labor whom we had anticipated being able to engage for the Hawaiian Islands." The warning was quickly fulfilled; shipments of Portuguese dwindled to 278 in 1885, and ceased altogether after 1888. Of the fourteen thousand Portuguese brought to the Hawaiian Islands, few returned to their native land; but, to the disappointment of the planters, very few were willing to renew their labor contracts at the expiration of the original

term.[1] They preferred to rent a bit of land and culti-
vate on their own account. The planters' loss was the
gain of the state. The Portuguese are to-day the small
farmer class and the backbone of the coffee industry.

A HUNT FOR LABORERS.

Other sources of supply had already been attempted.
The ever resourceful Gibson had proposed (1868) to secure Malaysians from the over-populated islands of the
Orient. Objections on the part of the Dutch government thwarted this enterprise, but for years to come the
hope that from Java and Sumatra might be derived a
population akin to the Hawaiian and capable of restor-
ing that decaying race hovered on the horizon as a
vision that might readily be realized. W. N. Armstrong, who accompanied Kalakaua on his journey
round the world in 1881, was commissioned to study
the labor possibilities of the countries visited. He once
and for all dispelled the Malay mirage by calling attention to the fact that the Malaysians were not the labor
reliance of the lands where they dwelt, and that the
Dutch government had been obliged to allow the importation of Chinese coolies. The reciprocity year saw
H. A. P. Carter sent to England to negotiate for the importation of East Indians as contract laborers. This
hopeful project was disapproved from the start by the
East Indian authorities, who successfully blocked negotiations. Persistent inquiry demonstrated that the
British government would consent to no scheme of emigration that did not provide for a first-hand supervision
of the laborers by protectors responsible to the Colonial
Office. This proviso effectually disposed of all hope of
Hindoo labor. A proposition to import negroes from the

[1] See Table B, p. 64.

southern states or from Kansas was considered by the
Board in 1880, and General Armstrong of the Hampton
Institute was requested to report upon its feasibility.[1]
The report was discouraging. The cost of transportation
would be great, and it was believed that the negro
would be quite unwilling to enter into any labor contract that might be penally enforced. The proposition
was finally set aside by a resolution of the Hawaiian
legislature disapproving the introduction of negro
laborers.

Some of the more public-spirited planters now turned
their attention to Europe as a possible recruiting ground.
In the lands where the climate was severe and nature
provided but a sparse subsistence, surely men might be
found willing, nay glad, to migrate to the " Paradise of
the Pacific." One hundred and twenty-four Germans,
men, women, and children, were imported as contract
laborers in 1880. They proved highly satisfactory as
laborers and as citizens, but they did not long remain
agriculturists. After serving out his three years' term,
a German readily found a position as *luna* or made his
way into a trade. It was not easy to secure further
shipments. The trend of emigration from Germany
was to the United States, where land might be had on
easy terms. Not more than fifteen hundred Germans in
all engaged for contract labor in Hawaii. In the same
year Castle and Cooke, enterprising merchants of Honolulu, obtained permission to import Scandinavians under
labor contracts. The Board agreed to pay half passage
for the women brought in and full passage for children.
Five hundred and fifty immigrants were the result of
this venture. They were readily placed on plantations,

[1] The actual investigation and report was made by W. N. Armstrong,
because General Armstrong was too much occupied to undertake it.

but hardly were they domiciled than furious protests were sent in to the Board and to the home government against the rations and quarters provided. The complaints showed a complete ignorance of the new living conditions. For example, the lack of butter and potatoes was regarded as a hardship. Butter and Irish potatoes were imported into the islands from San Francisco and were luxuries reserved to the tables of the rich. Further, the cottages were thought uninhabitable because between the roof and the siding was an interval of several inches. This means of ventilation is necessary to health in a plantation camp in Hawaii. The charges were promptly investigated by the Board and by a commissioner sent out by the Swedish government. The commissioner unhesitatingly pronounced the accusations frivolous and said that the people were faring far better than in the homes from which they came. They had been hastily recruited in the seaports and had no liking for agricultural labor. Their real grievance was that they were under contract to work for twenty dollars a month when they might have been earning from two to four dollars a day at various trades. Some of these laborers, absconding, carried their complaints to America and found there a more sympathetic audience. The San Francisco *Chronicle* in June, 1881, published a sensational article on the "modern slavery" permitted in the Hawaiian Islands. English and German papers copied the statements, and a new horror was exploited by the European press. A vigorous refutation was drawn up and signed by one hundred and six German residents in the islands. " Personal freedom is, thanks to a well-regulated legislation, as secure here as in those countries which claim the highest civilization, and the legal decrees concerning the relation between employer and working-man are entirely just and founded on those now in existence in the United States of America."

OPPOSITION TO THE CHINESE.

Meantime the importation of Chinese coolies went on apace. Laborers were always to be had in unlimited quantity and on easy terms from that swarming hive of men. In 1875 the legislature had attached a rider to the appropriation for the encouragement of agriculture and immigration, stipulating that no part of the sum should be used for the transportation of Chinese, excepting the bonus on women imported. But coolies continued to be brought in by private parties with the more or less reluctant consent of the Board of Immigration. The number rose from 62 in 1875 to 3652 in 1880 and to 4295 in 1884. By 1886 the Chinese in the islands numbered twenty thousand, one-fourth of the total population, but only 5605 of these were plantation laborers. The emancipated coolies found their way into various trades. Some were small shop-keepers, some had rented land and were cultivating rice and vegetables, many were earning good wages at diverse skilled trades. Serious as were the objections to the Chinese on moral grounds, they were highly satisfactory as workmen—peaceable, intelligent and reliable. Moreover, they cost less than the other laborers available.[1]

[1] The comparative cost of the several races represented on the plantations was estimated in the report of the Board of Immigration for 1886 as follows :—

	Cost of Importation	Aver. Wages (with Food)	Living Expenses
Portuguese	$112.00	$10.41 per mo.	$ 9.16 per mo.
Norwegians	130.00	9.00 "	10.00 "
Germans	100.00	12.75 "	8.00 "
Japanese[2]	65.85	9.88 "	6.32 "
Chinese	76.83	13.56 "	6.43 "
South Sea Islanders	78.50	10.16 "	5.77 "

[2] See pp. 42 and 43.

4

The initial expense of transportation was considerably less than for European laborers, and John Chinaman had few women and children to be provided for.

Public sentiment finally over-mastered the wishes of the planters. Agitation against the importation of Chinese was strong in the early eighties. Public-spirited Hawaiians protested against their vices, as a corrupting element in the body politic. Artisans complained that their competition was lowering wages and the standard of living. But the menace to public health involved in importing shiploads of orientals was perhaps the argument that told most heavily against them. In 1881 the *Septima* arrived at Honolulu with six hundred and ninety-nine Chinamen aboard and six cases of smallpox. The passengers were detained in quarantine, the sick being removed, until all danger of further out-break had passed. Soon after these men had been placed on plantations several other tramp steamers arrived in similar plight. The ordinary quarantine accommodations proved entirely inadequate, and the suspects were housed in make-shift quarters with a guard to prevent their escape. Complaints were forwarded to the Chinese Minister at Washington alleging that the coolies had been confined within a a stockade guarded by soldiers and so forced to sign contracts prejudicial to their interests. The old scandals concerning slavery in Hawaii were revived, much to the chagrin of all patriotic citizens.

In 1883 the first legislative restriction on the importation of Chinese was imposed. No more than six hundred were to be admitted in any consecutive three months, and they were to be transported in no vessels but those of the two regular lines, the Pacific Mail and the Oriental and Occidental. These restrictions were resented by the planters and a protest was addressed to the Minister of the Interior by the Planters' Association on August 27, 1884.

"The petition of the undersigned planters and other employers of labor respectfully represents that their several business enterprises are suffering in consequence of the scarcity of suitable laborers to perform the necessary work which their several business enterprises require and demand. And by reason of scarcity of the laborers, wages for unskilled labor, field hands, etc., are so high that the planters and other employers, under existing adverse circumstances, cannot afford to pay the ruling rate of wages, and consequent disaster threatens their several enterprises.

" And as the Chinese are acknowledged to be the best and most economical laborers in the kingdom for general plantation and other work, and knowing that additional numbers of Chinese in the kingdom would materially relieve the existing difficulties :

" Therefore, your petitioners pray that it may please Your Excellency to encourage, and as far as possible, provide for and allow a further and free immigration of Chinese from China and elsewhere into this Kingdom, to the number of 500 adult men per month, until all demands of labor shall be fully supplied.

" The intention of this petition is not to interfere with or check the immigration of Portuguese, Japanese or others, which people can be employed at other and higher classes of work, and thereby earn the higher rates of wages paid them."

A struggle between the planters and the press ensued, the former representing the industrial and the latter the social interests of the islands. Mindful of the fact that the prosperity of the sugar plantations was fundamental to the prosperity of all other business, the government provided against an actual shortage of labor by negotiating for a liberal importation of Japanese. Three thousand contract laborers were imported and a labor convention with Japan concluded in anticipation of more drastic legislation against the Chinese. The decade from 1885 to 1895 saw no less than four enactments on the vexed question of Chinese immigration. A law of 1885 prohibited any shipmaster from bringing in more than twenty-five Chinese who could not show pass-ports proving previous residence in the Hawaiian Islands. In 1886 was passed an exclusion act quite as rigid as the Geary law. "No Chinese passenger shall be allowed to land at any port in the Hawaiian Kingdom unless such passenger be the bearer of a pass-port" proving previous residence. The only exceptions allowed were merchants, for a limited term, wives and children of resident Chinese, officials representing the Chinese government, teachers, and ministers of the gospel.

In September, 1889, a committee of the planters petitioned the ministry to convene an extra session of the legislature to consider an amendment to the constitution making provision whereby "Chinese might be admitted to the Islands as plantation laborers and whereby Chinese so admitted and Chinese now in the country and employed as common laborers might be restricted to agriculture." The petition was refused on the ground that such an amendment had already been voted down. The ministerial policy was then stated as follows: "First, the excessive proportion of Chinese in the Kingdom and their rapid encroachment upon the various businesses and employments of the country, require adequate measures to prevent the speedy extinction

in these Islands of Western civilization by that of the
East, and the substitution of a Chinese for the Hawaiian
and other foreign population.   Second, the perpetuation
of Anglo-Saxon civilization, introduced into these
Islands and adopted by the Hawaiian people early in
the present century, is essential to the continuance of a
free government and of the political independence of
this Kingdom, and such civilization can be perpetuated
only by retaining a population who have been educated
therein and who comprehend the workings and benefits
of popular representative government.   Third, we be-
lieve that self-preservation, by nations as well as by
individuals, is a principle universally recognized."
Reviewing the policy of other nations, the ministry
undertook to justify by analogy the restrictions imposed
by the Hawaiian government on the immigration of
Chinese.   The United States had excluded such immigrants ; Canada and the Australian Colonies had imposed
restrictions ; the islands of the Pacific, the Philippines,
Samoa and Tahiti, had taken measures to protect themselves against Chinese competition ; in Java and the
Straits Settlements hostile legislation was imminent.
A statistical study of the situation in Hawaii followed,
and it was demonstrated that Chinese competition meant
the speedy substitution of the oriental for the native or
European workmen.   The Chinese in the Kingdom
then amounted to one-fifth of the entire population,[1]
having increased from 5916 in 1878 to 19,217 in 1889 ;
but the number employed as plantation laborers had not

[1] Proportion of Chinese in total population :—

1866	1.94%
1872	3.41
1878	10.20
1884	22.27
1889 (estimated)	20.88

increased in the interval.[1]   There was abundant evidence to show that the majority of the Chinamen who elected to remain in the islands at the expiration of their contracts had gone into various trades.[2]   The cabinet declared its conviction that the presence of Chinamen was a menace not only to the industrial but to the social well-being of the islands.   Their immorality, their secretiveness, their apparent disregard of human life, their imperviousness to western ideas were dwelt upon with much earnestness.[3]   After this extensive preamble it is somewhat disconcerting to find the cabinet arriving at a conclusion practically identical with that of the planters :
" 1.   That no Chinese other than teachers and officials shall be allowed to come into this country except in the capacity of laborers.   2.   That no Chinese be admitted

[1] Number of plantation laborers in Hawaii :—

	Chinese	All Nations
1882	5,037	10,243
1886	5,605	14,518
1888	5,727	15,578
1890	4,517 (later figures)	17,895

[2] In 1889 the Chinese held

10.9	per cent. of drivers' licenses.
18.2	" " draymens' "
20.6	" " butchers' "
23.5	" " wholesale merchandise licenses.
27.9	" " hack "
38.2	" " horse hiring "
57.0	" " wholesale spirit "
62.0	" " retail merchandise "
84.7	" " victualing "
91.8	" " pork butchers' "
100.0	" " cake-peddling "

[3] Ratio of convicted criminals to race population by two year periods, from the reports of the Chief Justice :—

	1891 and 1892	1896 and 1897	1901 and 1902
Chinese	9.86%	17.36%	12.8%
Japanese	7.31	7.94	7.7
Hawaiians	8.04	7.85	10.1
Portuguese	5.58	3.49	6.1
Others	10.73	12.44	24.0

as laborers unless the agricultural necessities of the
country require it. 3. That Chinese not now engaged
in trade or the mechanical occupations be prohibited
from hereafter engaging therein."

The representations of the planters prevailed with the
next legislature so far as to secure the admission of
Chinese as agricultural laborers for a term not exceeding
five years.   If found in any other occupation such
immigrants were to be arrested and returned to China.
The planter engaging such laborers must make a deposit
of $75 for each laborer, to be deducted from his monthly
wages. This was reserved by the board of immigration
to meet the expense of his return passage. In 1895 a
further modification of the Exclusion Act was allowed·
Permits to import Chinese coolies might be granted to
an employer who bound himself to introduce European
or American agricultural laborers equal in number to
one-tenth of the Chinese permitted him. This was to
be accomplished within one year after the date of the
permit. Such European or American laborers were to
be accompanied by women in the ratio of twenty-five
women to one hundred men. The government was to
defray the passage of women and children to the amount
of $130 per family; the planter was to defray the pass-
age of the men and any surplus for women and children.
A good and sufficient bond was required for the performance of this obligation. In the next two years
7364 Chinese were brought in under this arrangement.
Another immediate consequence of this legislation was
a renewed effort to obtain European laborers.   Two
hundred and twenty-seven Germans were imported in
1897, and 255 Italians in the year following, together
with as many Galicians from Austro-Hungary. These
efforts were rather perfunctory; the laborers so intro-

duced were but poor material and meant nothing as a solution of the labor problem.

THE JAPANESE.

The significant achievement of these years of agitation was the negotiation of the convention with Japan by which an important labor supply was opened up. In 1879 the Board had appropriated $10,000 for the introduction of laborers from Japan, and the Hawaiian consul at Tokio was instructed to submit the following terms to the Japanese government: Laborers coming to Hawaii were to enter into contract to work on a sugar plantation for a term of from three to five years. Wages were guaranteed at the rate of ten dollars per month for men and six dollars per month for women. Forty per cent of the immigrants were to be women, and the Board was to pay half the expenses of the passage of the women and all expenses for the children brought in. The people were to be returned at government charge if, at the end of the contract years, they did not wish to remain in Hawaii. These terms were sufficiently generous, but the Japanese authorities demurred. They were willing that the people should emigrate to Hawaii, but expressed themselves as decidedly adverse to any scheme of contract labor that seemed likely to place Japanese subjects in a position " similar to that of the Chinese in Peru, Cuba, or even California." There followed a remarkable " higgling of the market," the board of immigration eagerly meeting demand after demand of the wary Japanese officials. It was finally agreed that free passage to and from Japan should be provided for the laborers, their wives and children, that they should be guaranteed employment without signing an advance labor contract, and that the minimum rate

of wages, fixed before sailing, should be nine dollars per
month with food or fifteen dollars without food. The
board promised to provide laborers in the latter case
with standard rice at five cents a pound.

At last (February, 1885) the first shipment of Japanese
coolies was received—616 men, 159 women, and 108
children. Instructions as to treatment were embodied
in a circular letter to the planters : " The understanding
with the Japanese government is that while the immigrants remain under their original contracts they are to
be under the immediate guardianship of the government,
and that the planters to whom their contracts are
assigned are the agents of the government, the latter
being really responsible on the original contracts at all
points. It has further been distinctly considered and
determined by the government that no employer or
overseer [*luna*] shall be permitted under any circumstances (except in self-defense) to strike or lay hand
upon any contract laborer who is a government ward.
This determination is made binding by agreements to
this effect, actually entered into ; and it is rendered all
the more important when considered in the light of the
sensitive nature of the Japanese race, in particular,
which renders any rough handling of the laborer abor-
tive, if intended to secure obedience. It must therefore be understood by all employers that blows or other
violence used against a contract laborer, except in absolute self-defense, will be deemed sufficient ground for
the withdrawal of the assignment made to them of any
person so dealt with." A special commission of inspection of Japanese laborers was created with a Japanese
as chief and with interpreters for each island where
Japanese were employed, charged with the investigation
and amicable settlement of disputes that might arise

between laborer and employer.[1] The function of these interpreters was at first resented by the planters, but they proved so helpful in obviating difficulties that the plan was in the end heartily approved.

The ambition of the government to settle the labor problem once and for all by inducing " the voluntary immigration of a friendly people " seemed about to be realized. Of 3457 Japanese brought into Hawaii in the next three years (1885–1888), 2431 elected to remain under a second contract, 632 remained as free laborers, 291 returned to Japan, and the remainder died in the islands. The arrangement was regarded with such satisfaction by the Japanese government that propositions for a convention fixing the conditions of this immigration were favorably received.[2] The year 1886 saw the negotiation of a convention between the Empire of Japan and the Kingdom of the Hawaiian Islands.[3]

[1] A similar commission for the inspection of Portuguese, with a corresponding staff of interpreters, was established at the same time. Both commissions were to be under the direction of an inspector general responsible to the board of immigration. Quarterly reports were to be submitted to the board giving a detailed account of the condition of the laborers on each plantation.

[2] Propositions to recruit laborers for the United States and for Australia had been refused by the same government.

[3] Article II. The government of His Majesty the Emperor of Japan agree that in pursuance of the provisions of this convention, and so long as the same shall remain in force, Japanese subjects may freely emigrate to the Hawaiian Islands. But nothing herein contained shall be held to deprive His Imperial Majesty's government of the right, in individual cases, to prohibit such emigration, or at their pleasure generally to limit, suspend, or prohibit such emigration, if in their judgment the exigencies of the state or the welfare of the Japanese subjects justifies such action.

Article III. All emigration under this convention shall be carried on between the ports of Yokohoma and Honolulu. The Kenrei of Kanagawa shall in all matters connected therewith represent and act on behalf of the Japanese government. His Hawaiian Majesty's gov-

Sixty-two thousand Japanese were brought into the Hawaiian Islands under this convention, twenty-five per cent of them being women. As may be inferred from the insistent demand of the planters for Chinese laborers, the Japanese were not entirely satisfactory. From the outset they were difficult to deal with, proving to be restless and self-assertive to a degree hitherto unknown in the cane-fields of Hawaii. They were, more-

ernment engage to appoint a special agent of the Hawaiian Board of Immigration to reside at Yokohoma. The appointment of such agent shall be subject to the approval of the Japanese government. It shall be the duty of the said agent to correspond and consult with the said Kenrei upon all matters connected with the subject of Japanese emigration to Hawaii, and he shall, moreover, be charged with the duty of making all necessary arrangements with reference to the embarkation and transportation of intending emigrants. Whenever emigrants are desired, the said agent shall give the said Kenrei at least one month's previous notice, setting forth the number and class of persons desired, to which notice the said Kenrei shall, without unnecessary delay, reply, giving the determination of His Imperial Majesty's government in that behalf.

Article IV. All emigration under this convention shall be by contract. The contracts shall be for periods not exceeding three years, and shall be in accordance with a form to be approved by both governments. During the continuance of any such contracts, the Hawaiian government shall assume all the responsibilities of employer toward the emigrants and shall consequently be responsible for the due and faithful performance of all the conditions of such contracts and at the same time the said government of Hawaii guarantees to each and every Japanese emigrant the full and perfect protection of the laws of the Kingdom and will endeavor at all times and under all circumstances to promote the welfare and comfort of such emigrants.

Article V. His Hawaiian Majesty's government agrees, moreover, to furnish all emigrants under this convention free steerage passage, including proper food, from Yokohoma to Honolulu, in first class passenger steamers. The steamers selected for the purpose of transporting such emigrants shall be approved by the Kenrei of Kanagawa.

Article VI. In order to ensure the proper fulfillment of the terms of the contracts entered into between the Board of Immigration of the Hawaiian Kingdom and any Japanese emigrants and to afford full protection to such emigrants in the enjoyment of their rights under the laws of the Hawaiian Kingdom, His Hawaiian Majesty's government will provide and employ, during the continuance of any of the

over, remarkably clannish, clubbing together for the
championship of their common interests in a way that
was distinctly embarrassing. They showed no disposition to marry with the Hawaiians, and, while readily
adopting American dress and ways, cherished allegiance
to their native land with peculiar tenacity. They found
their way into the skilled trades even more rapidly than
the Chinese.[1] The danger that Hawaii might be orien-
talized was greater than in the days of unstinted Chinese

contracts aforesaid, a sufficient number of interpreters and inspectors
who shall be able to speak and interpret the Japanese and English
languages, and the services of such interpreters shall at all times be
rendered without charge to such emigrants in the courts of the Hawaiian Kingdom in any suits arising out of or concerning any such
contracts in which such emigrants may be plaintiffs, defendants, com-
plainants or accused.

Article VII. The government of His Hawaiian Majesty will, during
the continuance of any of the contracts provided for by this convention, employ a sufficient number of Japanese physicians to attend the
emigrants and will give to the said physicians the status of government physicians and will station them in such localities as may from
time to time appear to be desirable in order to afford the emigrants all
necessary medical aid.

Article VIII. His Hawaiian Majesty's government further agree
that the Diplomatic and Consular agents of Japan in Hawaii shall at
all times have free and unrestricted access to all Japanese emigrants,
they shall be afforded every facility to satisfy themselves that the contracts are being fulfilled in good faith ; and they shall also have the
right, in case of violation thereof, to ask and obtain the protection of
the laws and the local authorities of Hawaii.

Article IX. The well-being, happiness and prosperity of Japanese
subjects emigrating to Hawaii, being equally objects of solicitude to
both contracting parties, His Imperial Japanese Majesty's government
consent that His Hawaiian Majesty's government shall have the right
to send back to Japan all evil-disposed, vicious or vagrant Japanese
subjects in Hawaii, who may create trouble or disturbance or encourage dissipation of any kind among the emigrants or who may become
a charge upon the state.

[Signed]   WALTER M. GIBSON,
                           Minister of Foreign Affairs.

[1] According to the last census of occupations for Hawaii the Japanese
furnish 103 out of 399 blacksmiths ; 649 out of 1955 carpenters ; 386
out of 506 sugar mill hands ; 207 out of 383 seamstresses.

immigration. In fact the fear that the islands would be annexed by Japan was one of the prime factors in the demand for annexation to the United States.

INDUSTRIAL EFFECTS OF ANNEXATION.

The industrial transformation wrought by annexation was far more profound than the political. The immediate legislative consequences were the exclusion of Chinese laborers and the prohibition of the penal enforcement of labor contracts.[1] The absolute exclusion of the Chinese had been anticipated, as had also the prohibition of the further importation of contract laborers. But it had been supposed that existing contracts would hold to the expiration of the stipulated terms. Indeed the planters had imported an unusually large number of Japanese (19,908 in 1899) in anticipation of prohibitory legislation. The immediate effect of the marshal's proclamation was an epidemic of strikes. Of the twenty-two strikes recorded by the United States labor commissioner for 1900, twenty were undertaken by plantation laborers, all of them Japanese. The causes given throw a good deal of light on the aspirations of the inscrutable Jap: "for discharge of over-seer"; "for in-

[1] By the Organic Act (1900) providing a government for the territory of Hawaii it was stipulated that " no suit or proceedings shall be maintained for the specific performance of any contract heretofore or hereafter entered into for personal labor or service, nor shall any remedy exist or be enforced for breach of any such contract except in a civil suit or proceeding instituted solely to recover damages for such breach. Provided further that the provisions of this section shall not modify or change the laws of the United States applicable to merchant seamen. Contracts made since August 12th, 1898, by which persons are held for service for a definite term, are hereby declared null and void and terminated, and no law shall be passed to enforce said contracts in any way ; and it shall be the duty of the United States marshal to at once notify such persons so held of the termination of their contracts."

crease of wages, increase of water supply at dwellings,
payment of damages for injuries received by an employee,
and against retention of part of wages withheld in accordance with original contracts " ; " for cancellation of
contracts " ; " against being compelled to work regular
hours " ; " for increase of wages from $17.50 to $26 per
month " ; " for reinstatement of discharged employee " ;
" for employment of Japanese instead of white overseer ";
" against the task system " ; " against being compelled to
work on holidays." This sudden advent of full-blown
trade-unionism took the planters by surprise. For the
moment the laborers had the upper hand. But under
the auspices of the Planters' Association a uniform scale
of wages was soon agreed upon by which all the managers were to abide. The monthly wage for field labor
was fixed at $18, $19, and $20, according to the dis-
tance from the nearest town. This advance represents a considerable increase in cost of production.[1]
The immigration of Japanese did not cease with the
abolition of labor contracts.[2] The Hawaiian Islands
still offer opportunity for earning good wages under
congenial skies and a chance to rise in the world. The
conditions of immigration are altered, however. Passage

[1] In 1898 the Planters' Association submitted a memorial to the Hawaiian Commission in which the cost of labor is discussed as follows :
" Contrary to usual comment and understanding in the United States,
the average cost of ordinary field labor in Hawaii, counting in the
lodgings, medical attendance, wood, water, and land for cultivation
almost universally furnished to the laborers, does not in any case fall
below $16 per month, in most cases comes to as high as $18 a month
and ranges up to $20 and even more a month." This statement is
corroborated in the report of the U. S. commissioner of labor, on
Hawaii, 1902. Mr. Clarke's comparison of labor conditions in the
sugar industry of Hawaii, California, Texas, Louisiana, and Cuba
demonstrates the advantage of the Hawaiian laborers.

[2] The number of Japanese immigrants arriving in 1901 was 7,214 ; in
1902, 14,564.

money is usually advanced by immigration companies,[1] chartered by the Japanese government, which exact a bond for repayment from the immigrant or from his relatives. In case a man absconds the sum deposited is confiscated to the treasury of the company. The government reserves full right to limit the number of laborers who may be recruited and the towns or districts from which they may be drawn.[2]

THE PRO AND CON OF CONTRACT LABOR.

Much misunderstanding has arisen concerning this method of meeting the labor demand of the sugar planters. The evil reputation of the coolie trade—a reputation well-earned in Cuba and in the Chincha Islands— has attached itself to every attempt to transfer the superabundant population of Asia to the lands where their labor is in demand. It must be acknowledged that the penal enforcement of a labor contract is inconsistent with the trend of modern labor legislation. It suggests slavery. But how otherwise could the laborer, guiltless of property and in debt for his passage money, secure his master against breach of contract? The labor contract, moreover, was the only practical method of securing labor in a country so remote from the sources

[1] Article III of the Imperial Law for protecting emigrants :—
The Executive Authorities may cause imin (the emigrants) desiring to emigrate without the intervention of Imin Toriatskainin (emigration agents) to appoint sureties of not less than two persons whom they deem proper, according to the conditions of the place where they desire to emigrate. Such sureties shall give assistance to or undertake to bring home the imin in case of illness or other distress. In case the Executive Authorities shall have given assistance to or undertaken to bring home the imin, the sureties shall reimburse the expenses incurred therefore.

[2] A revision of the emigration laws, January 1, 1903, restricted the number of emigrants to Hawaii, an average of forty-five men to each of the thirty-five emigration agencies being allowed.

of supply. Laborers could be induced to immigrate only by the offer of passage prepaid and a guarantee of employment at a living wage. Planters could not be expected to meet these terms unless they were guaranteed against loss by a legal claim on the laborer for a definite term. Finally social security would have been threatened by the importation of alien laborers in numbers far exceeding the native population, but for the fact that these men were held upon the plantations by the labor obligation.

At a citizens' meeting called in 1869 to discuss the labor question the president of the Board of Immigration thus defended the government against the charge of countenancing " man-stealers " and " slavers " : " You cannot bring laborers here without first making a contract to pay certain wages and to provide food and lodging,— these are the inducements for them to come, and the government must hold out these inducements or they would not come,—whether Chinese or others. Under our laws all are alike. There is nothing like slavery here, and immigration cannot be made freer than it is." In his report of 1886, Charles Gulick, president of the Board, summing up a comprehensive review of the immigration policy of the Hawaiian government asserts : " The coolie system known as such has never existed here. The only law between employer and employee is the Master and Servant Law, than which none is milder or more equitable, requiring as it does the specific fulfillment of contracts. The law protects the laborer in all his rights, and affords no more protection to employers in theirs."

Contract labor as practiced in the Hawaiian Islands was fully justified by the peculiar social and industrial conditions there prevailing. As administered by the

Board of Immigration, the system was calculated to advance the interests of the laborers quite as much as
those of the planters. That it has done so is evident
from the property statistics of the twelfth census. The
value of the farm lands in which Chinese are interested
as owners, part owners, managers, cash-tenants, or share-
tenants is $2,700,335. The Japanese have had less
time in which to acquire property, but their interest is
estimated at $438,020. The Chinese residents in the
Hawaiian Islands pay taxes on $3,287,802 of personal
property, the Japanese on $1,268,180. It would not be
difficult to prove that for the oriental laborer the labor
contract has been the highroad to fortune.

The importation of thousands of orientals under a
semi-servile labor contract had, however, a discouraging
effect on free immigration. In so far, the Hawaiian
labor system is quite comparable to the slave labor system of the southern states. This tendency has been
recognized and deplored by all public spirited citizens
of the islands. In a memorial addressed to the Hawaiian
Commission in 1898 this attitude is stated as follows :
" The evils of the penal contract system and its
tendency to depreciate the standard of labor as an
honorable calling have been recognized and appreciated
by the great bulk of the intelligent people of Hawaii,
and it is almost entirely fallen into disuse, except with
relation to the newly imported immigrants and the securing of the advances made to and on account of them.
So great has been this tendency that the census of 1896 [1]
shows that of approximately 35,000 laborers only approximately 10,000 were working under contract and
these almost exclusively under contracts made abroad."

Much might be said in favor of the labor contract as

[1] *Cf.* Table B, p. 64.

5

a wholesome regulator of immigration. The normal demand for labor so expressed is a safer stimulant than the specious promises made by steam-ship and rail-road agents. Under a wise and efficient administration such as characterized the Hawaiian Islands and still obtains in British Guiana and the Strait Settlements, the mis-fits resulting from voluntary and unrestricted immigration have been largely avoided. The far more serious evils arising from an illicit importation of contract laborers as practiced by the Six Companies on our Pacific coast and by the Italian padrone can be obviated by government control.

The insuperable objections to the labor contract, appreciated to the full by the defendants of the system, is the difficulty of enforcement. How can the courts compel a man who has no property but his bodily energies to fulfil his contract and so meet the money obligations incurred in transportation? Obviously he has nothing to forfeit but his freedom. But is not penal enforcement inconsistent with personal liberty? This dilemma has been fully treated in two important rulings of the Hawaiian supreme court. In 1873 in the case of John H. Wood vs. Afo (*alias* Cheong San Quong), the court affirmed :—

" This statute [the Master and Servants Act] was enacted, of course, in reference to the business of the country. The productions of the country must be gathered and secured, or manufactured when secured, and if neglected they deteriorate and are essentially damaged, and the law in question is designed to prevent persons from wilfully violating their contracts and doing damage to their employers. It is, in degree, as essential to the sugar planter that his employees should remain with him to perform the service as agreed upon during the

crop, as it is for the seaman to remain on the ship during the voyage.   A sugar plantation encounters as many
adverse winds as a vessel, and is quite as likely to be en-
dangered in crop time as a vessel is on a lee shore, when
all hands are required.   In many countries where labor
is plenty and heavy advances are not necessary to pro-
cure laborers, this law is not necessary.   But the legislature, in their wisdom, passed the law as applicable to
the condition of affairs here.

" But it is contended that it is in restraint of one's liberty,—why more so than any other contract which a
man makes and honestly fulfills ?   If a mechanic under-
takes to build a house, it occupies his time and diverts
his attention from other pursuits, which, perhaps, he
might prefer.   Every man in public office is under
obligation to attend to its duties, and it is often in
restraint of his wishes, but no one thinks it impairs
his liberty.   The court is of the opinion that it is im-
moral to fail to fulfill a contract without reason.   The
man when he makes the contract understands perfectly
well its terms, and receives advantages in advance, and
if fully complied with, how is his liberty interfered
with ?   It was optional whether he made the contract
or not, but when he has made it and received part payment, it is not true liberty regulated by law for him to
abandon his obligations and defraud his employer out of
the money advanced.   But it is said, bring your action
for damages.   This may be regarded in most cases as
mere mockery.   It is to incur a bill of costs without the
slightest probability of receiving the amount awarded.
There would be some strength in the argument if the
damages could probably be secured, but the legislature,
in their wisdom, considered the necessities of the business done here as well as the condition, moral and phy-

sical, of the people who usually enter into contracts of this character."

Again in 1891 the court was called upon to decide upon the apparent inconsistency between penal enforcement and personal liberty. Mioshi, a Japanese under contract to the Board of Immigration and assigned to the Hilo Sugar Company, sued for exemption on the ground that the contract was a violation of the constitution, since he was unwilling to serve, and Article XI of the constitution of 1864 and 1887 prohibit "involuntary servitude."[1] The judges ruled that the contract was constitutional. "Article XI was enacted while the Master and Servants Act was in full force, hence it could not have contemplated contracts to labor voluntarily undertaken. A fair and honest contract to work for another, willingly and freely made with a knowledge of the circumstances, cannot be said to have created a condition of involuntary servitude. The contract which creates the state or condition of service, if it is voluntary when made and the conditions and circumstances remain unchanged, except that the mind of the one who serves is now unwilling to fulfill it, is it not by that fact changed into a contract of involuntary servitude forbidden by law. If the contract is lawful and constitutional in its inception, it does not become illegal or unconstitutional at the option of the parties."

Quite in accordance with this ruling is the act of the legislature of 1892 reenforcing the penalties for desertion from service. If the servant refused to serve he was to be imprisoned until he consented. If he returned but again deserted, he could be fined not ex-

[1] Involuntary servitude, except for crime, is forever prohibited in this Kingdom. Whenever a slave shall enter Hawaiian territory he shall be free."

ceeding five dollars for the first offence and not exeeding ten dollars for the second offence, and in default of payment of the fine be imprisoned at hard labor until it was paid. For every subsequent offence he might be imprisoned at hard labor not exceeding three months and he must then serve the remainder of his original term.

CONTRACT LABOR SUPERSEDED.

By annexation to the United States, Hawaiian institutions were brought under direct control of a people accustomed to express their notions of individual liberty in legislation. Doubtless ignorance and prejudice were mingled in the popular discussion of the terms on which the islands should become an integral part of our government ; but the denunciation of contract labor had its origin in the conviction that the penal enforcement of a personal obligation is inconsistent with democracy, that it belongs not to the future but to the past, that it must go the way of those other forms of forced labor, slavery and serfdom. The history of labor systems in America goes far to justify this point of view. Indentured servants ceased to be brought into the Atlantic colonies before the close of the eighteenth century. Slavery was abolished in 1863. The importation of contract laborers was rendered illegal by the law of 1885, and all engagements made in advance of landing in this country were declared void.

A similar tendency is evident in European legislation. In England desertion of service on the part of artisans and servants in husbandry was treated as a crime for centuries, and a long series of statutes from 23 Edward III to 4 George IV prescribed penalties of mediæval severity. As late as 1866 a servant refusing to labor till the end of his term might be imprisoned at hard

labor in a house of correction or suffer abatement of
wages, as the magistrate might direct. But the masters'
right of penal enforcement was destined to give way before the people's demand for personal liberty. The year
that gave the suffrage to the ten pound householder
witnessed an important modification of the Master and
Servants Act. In accordance with the recommendations
of a select committee of the House of Commons
(1867) fine was substituted for imprisonment as a
penalty for non-performance except where injury to the
master's person or property could be proved. In 1875 a
second parliamentary commission made an exhaustive
report on the vexed question of the enforcement of labor
contracts. For the Master and Servants Act was then
substituted the Employers and Workmen Act, by which
the laborer was permitted to give security for due performance in lieu of paying a fine. Germany was the
last of the continental states to surrender the principle
of penal enforcement. The Prussian law of 1869
abolished the right of compulsion. No German laborer
may to-day be forced to resume his service, though he
may be sentenced to pay a fine for damage wrought.
Soldiers are not affected by this emancipating legislation, and the seaman's contract, even in the merchant
marine, may still be penally enforced in every European
port.

The seamen's union of the United States has waged
long and bitter war against this last stronghold of com-
pulsory service. Their contention has been carried to
the highest tribunals of the land with discouraging result. As late as 1896 the majority of the justices in the
Supreme Court sustained the shipping law. (Robert-
son vs. Baldwin, January 25, 1896.) The petitioners
had sued out a writ of habeas corpus by way of pro-

test against forcible detention on board ship as contrary
to the thirteenth amendment. The court affirmed in
the following terms the constitutionality of the penal
enforcement of the contract.

" The prohibition of slavery in the thirteenth amendment is well known to have been adopted with reference to a state of affairs which had existed in certain
states of the Union since the foundation of the government, while the addition of the words (involuntary
servitude) were said in the Slaughter-house cases [1873]
to have been intended to cover the system of Mexican
peonage and the Chinese coolie trade, the practical operation of which might have been the revival of the in-
stitution of slavery under a different and less offensive
name. It is clear, however, that the amendment was
not intended to introduce any novel doctrine with res-
pect to certain descriptions of service which have always been treated as exceptional, such as military and
naval enlistments.

" The question whether Sections 4598 and 4599 [the
penal sections of the Shipping Act] conflict with the
thirteenth amendment forbidding slavery and involuntary servitude, depends upon the construction to be giv-
en to the word (servitude). Does the epithet (involuntary) attach to the word (servitude) continuously,
and make illegal any service which becomes involuntary
at any time during its existence ? or does it attach only
at the inception of the servitude, and characterize it as
unlawful because unlawfully entered into ? If the former be the true construction, then no one, not even a
soldier, sailor, or apprentice can surrender his liberty,
even for a day ; and the soldier may desert his regiment
upon the eve of battle, or the sailor abandon his ship at
any intermediate port or landing, or even in a storm at

sea, provided only he can find means of escaping to another vessel.   If the latter, then an individual may, for
a valuable consideration, for a definite time, and for a
recognized purpose, contract for the surrender of his
personal liberty and subordinate his going and coming
to the will of another during the continuance of the
contract." Justice Harlan dissented : " Slavery exists
wherever the law recognizes a right of property in a
human being ; but slavery cannot exist in any form
within the United States.   The thirteenth amendment
uprooted slavery as it once existed in this country and
destroyed all of its badges and incidents.   It established
freedom for all."

The opinion of Justice Harlan was destined to pre-
vail.   On December 21, 1898, Congress passed an
amendment to the Shipping Act which provided that in
case of desertion from an American vessel in ports of
the United States and its dependencies, or in ports of
Canada, Newfoundland, the West Indies, and Mexico,
the seaman or apprentice so deserting should forfeit all
effects left on board and all wages due him.   Deserters
from an American vessel in a foreign port may suffer
the further penalty of three months imprisonment.   But
in the ports of the United States, her neighbors and
dependencies, the ship-master's right of bodily compulsion is finally abolished.

From the foregoing sketch of the tendencies in recent legislation, one must conclude that penal enforcement, the essential condition of contract labor, is an
anachronism in the modern industrial order and destined
everywhere to be superseded by a higher labor type.
Conditions in Hawaii are peculiar in that the abolition
of the penal contract was not demanded by the coolies
or by the planters, but was imposed by the United

States government as a condition of annexation. Public opinion in the United States demanded that the laborer in Hawaii should be as free as the laborer at home. Americans could not comprehend that in a tropical country worked by oriental labor the wage system might be an anachronism.

THE CONTRACT COMPANY.

The years immediately following the abolition of contract labor were full of difficulty for the Hawaiian sugar-planters. In 1895 the labor commission,[1] reporting on the problems then besetting the employer of labor, declared the wage relation a failure. " It is generally conceded by planters, in these islands and elsewhere, that the system of wage-paying is the least satisfactory of any of the forms of labor employment, because as the wages are the same, it does not stimulate the ambition of the laborer, and, indeed, tends to reduce the amount of labor furnished by each laborer to the product of the least efficient and most thriftless." This is especially true in the case of Japanese laborers, now seventy per cent of the total labor supply. As a race these men are restless, ambitious, and eager for change. In marked contrast to the patient, industrious Chinaman, the Japanese is quick to take offense, ready with his fists and altogether a difficult and unreliable employee. Under no pecuniary bond to his employer and attached to the plantation by no sense of loyalty or self-interest, he requires constant over-sight.

The old fashioned planter has fallen into despair. The more progressive men have hit upon a device that promises well. This is a form of rental similar to

[1] See Report of the Labor Commission on Coöperation and Profit sharing, 1895.

farming on shares, except that the lease is taken up not by an individual farmer but by a company of laborers. The planter furnishes land, seed-cane, water, fertilizer, and tools, and performs such portions of the work as require expensive machinery, *e.g.*, plowing, furrowing, and hauling the cane to mill. He also provides house, garden, and fuel to each laborer's family and advances him ten dollars per month towards living expenses. A field of from fifty to one hundred acres is rented to a " contract company" of a dozen or more men. Under a head-man of their own choosing, the co-laborers weed, irrigate, and fertilize the fields, strip and finally cut the cane and load it for transportation. The cane is weighed as it leaves the field or, when practical, reckoning is kept at the mill of the raw sugar produced from the crop in question, and each company is paid for its product at the rate stipulated in the contracts. This piece-price varies with the market price of sugar. Two dollars per ton of cane or seven dollars per ton of sugar is the present rate, approximately one-seventh of the total value of the crop.

The purchase system was in the experimental stage when the labor commission made the report above quoted. At that time the method had been tried on some eight plantations with varying degrees of success. Only four managers gave it unhesitating approval. To-day the purchase system is the usual method of dealing with Japanese laborers, since it is a relation that brings out their best qualities. The " contract company" at its best is a labor-gild, associated in the bond of a common interest. The jealous attention given to their cultivation of a crop shows in marked contrast to the perfunctory performance of hired laborers. The company men irrigate with careful attention to the quality of the soil, begging for more fertilizer than has been allotted them, stealing it from the ware-house in case of necessity. They go to the field in advance of the day-laborers and stay after hours, weeding or stripping or guarding against fire. The result, under the same conditions of soil and water supply, is a yield greater by one-fourth or one-fifth than the crop produced by the labor gang supervised by a *luna*. The planter reaps an enhanced profit, and the earnings of the men are twenty-five per cent more than they would receive as wage laborers. There is indeed good reason to hope that the purchase system will prove the ultimate solution of the labor problem in the Hawaii Islands.

TABLE A

IMMIGRATION INTO THE HAWAIIAN ISLANDS UNDER THE BOARD OF IMMIGRATION

YEAR	Chinese	Japanese	Portuguese	German	Galicians	Norwegians	South Sea Islanders	Total
1865	615						39	654
1866	117							117
1867	210							214
1868	51	148					4	325
1869	78						126	100
1870	305						22	330
1871	223						25	223
1872	61							61
1873	48							48
1874	62						7	69
1875	151							151
1876	1,283							1,283
1877	557							557
1878	2,464		180				214	2,868
1879	3,652		419				478	4,549
1880	2,422		332				793	3,547
1881	3,898		840			615	245	5,598
1882	1,367		2,356	183			21	3,927
1883	4,295		3,812	826			329	9,262
1884	2,693		1,532	18			120	4,363
1885	2,924	1,946	278	25			21	5,194
1886	338	979	467					1,784
87-88[2]		1,429[2]	239[2]					1,668[2]
88-90[2]		7,310[2]	343[2]					7,656[2]
90-92[2]	431[2]	9,511[2]						9,942[2]
92-94[2]	95[2]	6,095[2]						6,190[2]
1894[3]		1,486[3]						1,486[3]
95-97[2]	5,241[2]	6,454[2]		227[2]				14,972[2]
1898		9,768			372			10,090
1899	24	19,908	337					20,269
Total__	33,605	65,034	10,835	1,279	372	615	2,444	114,184

[1] Immigration of Chinese into the islands under the Royal Hawaiian Agricultural Society was as follows: 1852, 293; 1853, 64; 1854, 12; 1855, 61; 1856, 23; 1857, 14; 1858, 13; 1859, 171; 1860, 21; 1861, 2; 1862, 13; 1863, 8; 1864-9.

[2] Two years.

[3] Nine months.

TABLE B

Number and Nationality of Laborers on Plantations

1886	Men		Women	Children	Total
	Contract	Free			
Hawaiian _____	1,319	817	119	-----	2,255
Portuguese_____	1,846	609	444	182	3,081
Japanese_____	1,691	24	234	-----	1,949
Chinese_____	863	4,736	6	-----	5,605
German_____	194	66	67	-----	327
Norwegian_____	4	46	2	-----	52
Islanders_____	337	57	80	-----	474
Total_____	6,254	6,355	952	182	13,743
1896					
Hawaiian _____	399	1,186	30	-----	1,615
Portuguese_____	375	1,466	116	311	2,268
Japanese_____	6,497	5,518	878	-----	12,893
Chinese_____	4,374	1,915	-----	-----	6,289
Islanders_____	60	55	-----	-----	115
Germans_____	-----	169	-----	-----	169
Other nationalities ____	-----	117	-----	-----	117
Total_____	11,705	10,426	1,024	311	23,466
1899					
Hawaiian _____	163	1,125	38	-----	1,329
Portuguese_____	153	1,618	130	252	2,153
Japanese_____	17,547	5,741	2,366	-----	25,654
Chinese_____	2,768	3,201	-----	-----	5,969
Germans_____	-----	138	-----	-----	138
Scandinavians_____	-----	37	-----	-----	37
Austrians _____	-----	189	-----	-----	189
Other nationalities ____	-----	66	-----	-----	66
Total_____	20,631	12,115	2,534	252	35,184

	Total
1901	
Hawaiian_____	1,460
Portuguese _____	2,417
Japanese _____	27,531
Chinese _____	4,976
Porto Ricans_____	2,095
South Sea islanders _____	46
Other Nationalities_____	1,046
Total_____	39,587

TABLE C

PRODUCTION OF HAWAIIAN SUGAR PLANTATIONS IN POUNDS

Year	Pounds	Year	Pounds
1837	4,286	1870	18,783,639
1838	88,543	1871	21,760,773
1839	100,000	1872	16,995,402
1840	360,000	1873	23,129,101
1841 (6 months)	60,000	1874	24,566,611
1842		1875	25,080,182
1843	1,145,010	1876	26,072,429
1844	513,684	1877	25,575,965
1845	302,114	1878	38,431,458
1846	300,000	1879	49,020,972
1847	594,816	1880	63,584.871
1848	499,533	1881	93,789,483
1849	653,820	1882	114,177,938
1850	750,238	1883	114,107,155
1851	21,030	1884	142,654,923
1852	699,170	1885	171,350,314
1853	642,746	1886	216,223,615
1854	575,777	1887	212,763,647
1855	289,908	1888	235,888,346
1856	554,805	1889	242,165,835
1857	700,556	1890	259,789,462
1858	1,204,061	1891	274,983,580
1859	1,826,620	1892	263,636,715
1860	1,444,271	1893	330,822,879
1861	2,562,498	1894	306,684,993
1862	3,005,603	1895	294,784,819
1863	5,292,121	1896	443,569,282
1864	10,414,441	1897	520,158,232
1865	15,318,097	1898	444,963,036
1866	17,729,161	1899	545,370.537
1867	17,127,187	1900	344,531,173
1868	18,312,926	1901	690,882,132
1869	18,302,110		

TABLE D.

TABLE SHOWING WAGES OF CONTRACT LABORERS ON WAILUKU
PLANTATION FROM 1868 TO JUNE 14, 1900.

Year	Hawaiians.			Chinese.		South Sea Islanders.	
1868	$ 8.00 and $10.00 per mo.						
1869	8.00 " 10.00 "						
1870	8.00 " 10.00 "						
1871	8.00 " 10.00 "			$15.00 per mo.			
1872	8.00 " 10.00 "			15.00 "			
1873	8.00 " 10.00 "			15.00 "			
1874	8.00 " 10.00 "			15.00 "		$15.00 per mo.	
1875	9 00 " 10.00 "			15.00 "		15.00 "	
1876	9.00 " 10.00 "			14.00 "		14.00 "	
1877	9.00 " 10.00 "			14.00 "			
1878	10.00 to 13.00 "			14.00 "			
1879	10.00 " 13.00 "			17.50 "			
1880	10.00 " 13.00 "			17.50 "		16.00 to $18.00 "	
1881	12.00 " 15.00 "			15.50 "		16.00 " 18.00 "	
1882	13.00 " 16.00 "			15.50 "		16.00 "	
1883	15.00 " 16.00 "			15.50 "		16.00 "	
1884	13.00 " 16.00 "			15.50 "		13.00 " 14.00 "	
1885	13.00 " 15.00 "			15.00 "		13.00 " 14.00 "	
1886	13.00 " 15.00 "			15.00 "		13.00 " 14.00 "	
1887	13.00 " 15.00 "			15.00 "		15.00 "	
1888	13.00 " 15.00 "			15.00 "		15.00 "	
1889	14.00 " 16.00 "			17.00 "		14.00 " 15.00 "	
1890	14.00 " 16.00 "					14.00 " 15.00 "	
1891	14.00 " 16.00 "					14.00 " 15.00 "	
1892	14.00 " 16.00 "					14.00 " 15.00 "	
1893	13.00 " 15.00 "						
1894	12.00 " 13.00 "						
1895	11.00 " 12.00 "						
1896	11.00 " 12.00 "						
1897	11.00 " 12.00 "						
1898	11.00 " 12.00 "						
1899	11.00 " 12.00 "						

NOTES—All laborers furnished house, wood, water, medical attendance, taxes.
Natives received a bonus for contracting one year $15.00; two years $25.00.

TABLE D—*Continued.*

TABLE SHOWING WAGES OF CONTRACT LABORERS ON WAILUKU PLANTATION FROM 1868 TO JUNE 14, 1900.

Year.	Portuguese.	Spanish.	Norwegian.	Japanese.
1868	----	----	----	----
1869	----	----	----	----
1870	----	----	----	----
1871	----	----	----	----
1872	----	----	----	----
1873	----	----	----	----
1874	----	----	----	----
1875	----	----	----	----
1876	----	----	----	----
1877	$14 per m.	----	----	----
1878	14 "	----	----	----
1879	18 "	----	----	----
1880	18 ‥	$18 per m.	----	----
	18 "			
1881	9 and board " 8 " "	18 "	$9 and b'd pr. m.	----
1882	9 " " 8 " " 9 " "	18 "	9 " "	----
1883	8 " " 9 " "	18 "	9 " "	----
1884	8 " " 9 " "	18 "	----	----
1885	8 " " 18 "	----	----	{ $16.00 per m. { 9.00 and b'd "
1886	9 " " 8 " " 17 to 19 "	----	----	{ $16.00 " { 9.00 and b'd "
1887	9 and board " 8 " " 17 to 19 "	----	----	{ $15.00 to 16.00 " { 9.00 and b'd "
1888	9 and board " 8 " "	----	----	----
1889	17 to 18 "	----	----	----
1890	18 "	----	----	----
1891	18 "	----	----	$15.00 to $17.00 "
1892	----	----	----	15.00 " 17.00 "
1893	17 "	----	----	16.00 "
1894	17 "	----	----	12.00 "
1895	----	----	----	12.50 to 13.50 "
1896	----	----	----	12.50 " 13.50 "
1897	----	----	----	12.50 " 13.50 "
1898	----	----	----	12.50 " 13.50 "
1899	----	----	----	13.50 " 15.00 "

6

BIBLIOGRAPHY

Alexander, W. D., History of the Hawaiian people.
    Brief history of land titles.
Blackman, W. F., The making of Hawaii.
Jenkins, Edward, The Coolie, his rights and wrongs.
Ireland, A., Tropical colonization.
Jenks, J. W., English and Dutch colonies in the Orient.
Whitney, Caspar, Hawaiian America.
Hawaiian annual, 1875–1902.
Planters' Monthly, 1886–1902.
Reports of the board of immigration, 1882–1899.
Report of the Hawaiian commission, 1898.
Reports of the commissioner of labor on Hawaii, 1901 and 1902.
The Hawaiian codes, 1839, 1842, 1846, 1897.
Records of the Supreme Court of Hawaii.
Reports of the English parliamentary commissions on Master and Servants Act, 1867 and 1875.

For EU product safety concerns, contact us at Calle de José Abascal, 56–1°,
28003 Madrid, Spain or eugpsr@cambridge.org.